ORBIS CONNOISSEUR'S LIBRARY

SILVER

LUCINDA FLETCHER

ORBIS PUBLISHING LONDON

Contents

Designed and produced by Harriet Bridgeman Limited

© Istituto Geografico De Agostini, Novara 1973
English edition © Orbis Publishing Limited, London 1973
Printed in Italy by IGDA, Novara
SBN 0 85613 122 9

The destruction of European plate

In historical accounts of plate, the vast quantities used and the richness of the pieces described are astonishing. For example, Jean II of France, father of Charles V, had a throne of gold and a chair overlaid with silver, as well as a magnificent display of elaborate table-silver; Philippe le Bon, Duke of Burgundy, owned half a million ounces of silver plate and, on a more prosaic level, a young Parisian in 1392 wrote of his 'silver salt cellars for the high table, four great gilded goblets, four dozen hanaps [drinking vessels], four dozen silver spoons, ewers, alms mugs and sweetmeat dishes . . . .'

These accounts are tantalizing and frustrating for not only do very few early pieces survive but rarely are detailed descriptions of the vessels given, and much is left to the imagination. It is to pictures – early illuminations and later oil-paintings – that one must turn to get some idea of the stupendous richness of the past. In some early Flemish works, and more especially in seventeenth-century still-life subjects, curiosity is satisfied.

Silver has always been a precious commodity. Thus when fashioned into a piece for household use or show, great care is lavished upon it. But, equally, its value is frequently the cause of its destruction.

In the days before banks were established, the silver-smith would melt down coins to create a piece of silver which would be both useful and a comparatively safe means of guarding wealth: stolen coins, after all, might not be missed, whereas the absence of a sizeable piece of plate could quickly be discovered and, in times of need, the piece could be readily converted back into coinage. There was not then, as there is today, a sentimentality attached to old things; silver was frequently melted down merely in order to be remade in a more up-to-date style as fashions changed. It is no wonder that so much is lost to us now.

Not only did domestic crises claim the household plate, but national events led to its destruction. In England, supporters rallying to the aid of Charles I during the Civil War sacrificed much for his cause. It was at this time that many of the fabulous college collections at Oxford were destroyed. Previously, during the Reformation years, vast quantities of ecclesiastical plate – rich gothic chalices, gilded, enamelled and studded with precious stones – were broken up when Henry VIII dissolved those wealthy foundations, the monasteries. A lot of riches were directed into the King's pocket.

In France there was mass destruction, inevitably, during the Revolution years, and very little eighteenth-century French silver survives. Even before the Revolution, a lot of early French silver had already disappeared, for Louis XIV had ordered a mass melting-down of plate in 1689, 1700 and 1709 to pay the debts of his disastrous foreign wars. The crafty Saint-Simon wrote at the time: 'I was in the rear-guard. When I saw I was the only one of my rank eating off silver, I sent about a thousand pistoles worth to the Mint and locked up the rest'. Few can have been as wily. The destruction in Paris was massive and, as a result, little silver from before those times is still in existence today.

These are just a few instances in the depressing history of silver-destruction. Nonetheless, considering the political traumas and financial depressions which Europe has undergone over the years, it is amazing that the quantity to be seen today has been preserved at all.

Many of the early survivors are mounted pieces. They are made of some material such as coconut-shell, often of little value nowadays but originally highly prized, mounted on a silver stem or banded with silver straps. The actual weight of silver used upon them is slight and, as they were probably cups, bowls or flagons and served a useful purpose, they were barely worth destruction in times of stress. Clearly, silver was judged on its weight alone, the number of ounces being meticulously stated alongside inventory entries, and so it is mainly from these lightly mounted pieces that we have an indication of the rich taste of the period.

Medieval silver

Some of the materials mounted in silver were selected for their exotic colouring, strong colour being obviously much admired in medieval days. A large amount of silver was gilded by the mercury process, the finished product looking extremely rich: a mixture of gold and mercury was applied

Still-life with silver and pewter vessels by Gerrit Heda (c.1620–c.1702). (National Gallery, London)

to the finished article and heated until the mercury evaporated and the gold alone adhered. This was a successful process, although we know that many of the smiths suffered from the poisonous mercury fumes.

An attractive combination of silver and gold could be achieved by partial gilding, a technique known to us today as 'parcel gilding'. An advantage of gilding is that it prevents tarnishing and, as salt is very damaging to a silver surface, gilding was especially practical for those ceremonial stands in which it was contained.

A colourful decorative device was the insetting of precious or semi-precious stones. Pearls and garnets were especially popular and their high settings were elaborately and delicately worked. Enamelling was much employed also. The colours were either set into an incised field – the champlevé technique – or else wires were built up to form panel frames in the cloisonné process. Brilliant reds, greens and blues predominated.

The same techniques and the same style of decoration were shared by most of the countries of Europe during the gothic period. Extant pieces reveal a close dependence on gothic architecture. During the years when the great northern cathedrals were under construction, the metal-workers aped the patterns of the stonemasons: cusping, spiky fretwork, pinnacles and stiff-leaf ornament are all

delicately translated into silver. Lobing is a characteristic feature and many of the high stems of cups are interrupted by the addition of a faceted knop.

Renaissance silver

Of all the countries of Europe, Italy was least involved in the gothic movement. The pointed tracery patterns of the North were far removed from the rounded arches and domes of her classical heritage and, in the early fifteenth century, there began in Florence a conscious revival of Classicism which soon affected not only all the divided states of Italy but the other European countries as well.

There was, inevitably, a time-lag. The Renaissance was well under way in Italy before the rest of Europe was even aware of the movement. Countries such as Germany lacked the classical background of Italy and found it difficult to adapt to a style so at variance with the accepted Gothic. Besides, the Gothic was an art-form developed in the North, suited to both Northern temperament and Northern climate. It was a big step indeed to reject it in favour of a style imported from the South.

In turning to ancient Rome for inspiration, the renaissance silversmith could find little direct precedent upon which to model his work, for Roman silver had suffered the

4

		ENGLAND	
	⚓	**Birmingham**	
	👑	**Sheffield**	
🛡	🛡	**Chester**	
⊗	🛡	**Exeter**	
XX	🛡	**Newcastle**	
🏰	👑	**Norwich**	
⊕	🔵	**York**	
🛡	**H**	**Hull**	
🏰		**Bristol**	
		SCOTLAND	
🏰	🛡	**Edinburgh**	
	⬭	**Glasgow**	
INS		**Inverness**	
		IRELAND	
🛡	🛡	**Dublin**	
🏰		**Limerick**	

common fate of much metalwork with the passage of time. Like his Northern, gothic counterpart he drew on architecture and sculpture and reproduced the columns, friezes and pilasters of Antiquity. The scrolling patterns with which he ornamented his pieces were derived from the wall-paintings found in Roman houses that were being excavated. The rooms, silted over in the intervening years, appeared to be 'grottoes' and the name *groteschi* clung to the decoration found there which consisted of vine tendrils, curling acanthus leaves, cherubs, sphinxes and urns. The classical 'grotesque' was to provide a useful repertoire of ornament

Design for a hand-mirror by Etienne Delaune. 1561. (Ashmolean Museum, Oxford)

6

for succeeding generations of designers.

In the course of the fifteenth century, Italian silver achieved a balance and feeling for proportion inherent in most branches of the arts during this great age of artistic production. Although sculptural effects were achieved by casting, much of the plate had small-scale ornament and, if embossed (hammered out from the back), the decoration tended to be in low relief. In the succeeding century, however, silver was enlivened by a higher relief and an animated outline. The mannerist reaction led to a more hectic cluttering of ornament which was to be imitated and exaggerated in the North.

Among the great metalworkers of the sixteenth century

stands Benvenuto Cellini (1500–71). He is celebrated not only for his memoirs, written in 1558, and his treatizes on the goldsmith's art, sculpture and design, but also for his work for the French king, François I.

The French had become aware of the artistic situation in neighbouring Italy at the turn of the fifteenth century, when they mounted a military campaign there in order to regain territory around Naples. Acclimatized to extremes of Gothic, the French were nonetheless attracted to the Classicism which they saw there. It was during the reign of François I (1515–47) that the style became firmly rooted. Many Italians worked for this king, seeing in France a golden opportunity to gain the commissions that were becoming increasingly sparse in their native land. The painters Rosso and Primaticcio created the Long Gallery for him at Fontainebleau and Leonardo da Vinci settled at Amboise, where he died in 1519. In 1540, Cellini was commissioned to make his famous salt-cellar, now in the Kunsthistorisches Museum, Vienna.

This masterpiece is made of gold and richly decorated with colourful enamel. It was intended as a ceremonial piece to stand in a prominent position at the right hand of its owner at table. Although this is a particularly rich example, great care and skill were generally expended on these containers in an age when it was difficult to keep meat fresh and salt was a precious and necessary commodity.

The French were naturally deeply affected by the direct contact with Italy and their work is closer to renaissance ideals than that of contemporary German craftsmen. There, the over-decoration of German Gothic was carried on into the new, imported style, and it was some time before the Gothic was abandoned altogether in favour of Classicism; the two styles ran incongruously side by side for several decades.

Augsburg and Nuremberg were the great silver-working centres, the latter being the birth-place of the artist Albrecht Dürer in 1471. The son of a goldsmith, his influence is very marked upon the later productions of that town. In both cities, plate of great fineness was wrought, encrusted with delicate ornament and showing an inventiveness of design associated with the Gothic. Some cups were shaped like columbine flowers; others like terrestrial or celestial globes; like statuette groups of Diana hunting a stag or St. George confronting his dragon. Stags, lions and unicorns were represented and the appropriate animals chosen to form the bowls of cups commissioned by certain guilds: the Fishmongers' Guild of a town would probably boast a fish-shaped cup, for instance, while a bull would be considered apt for that of the Butchers.

Exotic shapes would be prompted by the wide variety of materials that were mounted; for example, an ostrich egg might compose the body of a silver-gilt swan or cockerel. Many of the most imaginative designs would be built around the curved form of the nautilus shell, which would often be pared down to its mother-of-pearl base and sometimes engraved as well.

German cups are often extremely tall, raised on stems shaped like the gnarled trunk of a tree or an Italianate urn. Additional height is given by a domed lid topped by an elaborately worked finial. Some knops are like vases full of flowers; others are miniature versions of the cups upon which they stand. Usually the bowl of a ceremonial cup is also highly ornamented, with strap-work, masks, and cherubs embossed or chased on the surface. Alternatively, lobing was a favourite device of the Germans, and a criss-cross 'pineapple' pattern was also popular. Engraving played an important role, and, frequently, the incised lines were filled with black 'niello' (a lead alloy) to emphasize the pattern. In many cases enamel was added, and yet another form of decoration consisted of an applied filigree web of silver.

A considerable amount is known about German silver, not only from the number of pieces that have survived since the sixteenth century, but also through the pattern-books of the day. Germany produced many designers whose work was circulated widely, thus spreading this quasi-gothic interpretation of the Renaissance to other countries. From Augsburg came Flötner, whose collection of woodcuts was issued between 1535 and 1541, while those of Virgil Solis were produced in Nuremberg. Erasmus Hornik had been trained in Antwerp and worked in Augsburg, Nuremberg and Prague producing a printed series of designs, and the famous Hans Brosamer published his work in Fulda.

From them much may be learnt of the fashions of the day. Clearly, the standing cup and cover was of primary importance, beakers and tankards being alternative drinking-vessels. The shallow, Italianate 'tazza' was used, and the ewer and basin appears to have been made in large numbers in those days, before the advent of the fork. Salts were generally low, circular or triangular and, strangely in that country of lavish display, never acquired the height of grandeur of their English equivalents.

Much of the silver flooding into Europe was mined in Spanish America. Spain was at the zenith of her power after the unification of 1492 and the sixteenth century witnessed extravagant expenditure on plate. In that great stronghold of Catholicism there was naturally particular emphasis on ecclesiastical silver and the vast sculptural *custodia* – towering monstrances carried in religious processions – are among the greatest works of the renaissance period.

The gradual transition from the gothic to the renaissance style (called the 'plateresque' style in Spain) may be traced in the work of that great silver-making family, the Arfes. Juan Arfe (1535–1603), the most famous, was responsible for the *custodia* of Seville, Avila and Valladolid. The last, made in 1590, is six and a half feet high and is generally considered his masterpiece. However, the golden days of Spanish prosperity were numbered; the shattering defeat of the Armada in 1588 was a setback to the country and Spanish silver entered upon a decline.

In the meantime, renaissance ideas had also filtered into England. Henry VIII (1509–47) vied with François I in his interpretation of the Italian Renaissance and a confrontation took place between the two monarchs in that amazing show of splendour, the Field of the Cloth of Gold, in 1520.

Like François, Henry imported Italian talent, but he neither succeeded in attracting such great names, nor brought about a widespread change in style. After the Reformation and Henry's break with the Church of Rome, renaissance theories continued to flood into England, but naturally, since political ties were now severed, they no longer came direct from Italy but via countries such as

Germany and Holland. Thus, England's Renaissance has a strongly Teutonic flavour.

Hans Holbein the Younger (1497–1543) played an important role in this. He paid his first visit to England in 1526, returning in the 1530s to become court painter to Henry. A versatile man, he dabbled in architecture and also designed silver. Several of his drawings still exist, showing the characteristic elaboration of his native town, Augsburg. One cup he designed, in 1536, was for Jane Seymour: it was destroyed in the seventeenth century, but we can get a clear picture of it from an inventory entry:

Item oone faire standing-Cup of golde, garnished about the Couer with eleven table diamoudes, and two pointed Diamoudes about the Cup Seventene table Diamoudes and one Pearle Pendent upon the Cupp, with theis words BOUND TO OBEY AND SERVE and H and I knitt together, in the Topp of the Cover the Queenes Armes, an Queen Janes Armes houlden by twoe Boyes under a Crowne Imperiall weighing Threescore and five ounces and a halfe.

When Holbein died in 1543, the flow of German influence was by no means stemmed, for Northern pattern-books continued to come into this country throughout the reign of Henry's daughter, Elizabeth I. No doubt German craftsmen worked in London and many German-made pieces were certainly imported. But confusion arises here, for not only are English and German pieces similar in form, but German pieces were frequently seen through the assaying procedure by an English smith. A foreign-made piece may thus bear an English hallmark.

Strict guild supervision was emerging in London as elsewhere in Europe. Silver was inspected, tested (to check that it was of the correct standard of silver-alloy content) and stamped accordingly at Goldsmiths' Hall, the Guild headquarters in the City of London. The stamp of guarantee ensured no crooked dealing on the part of smith or Company – an essential procedure in a trade all too open to fraudulent practices. The marks are very helpful as they enable a piece to be dated and attributed to a maker or town. By the middle of the sixteenth century, four marks were used in London – the town-mark in the form of a leopard's head, the lion passant as proof of sterling standard, the maker's mark and the date-letter.

Much surviving Elizabethan silver consists of mounted pieces incorporating the same materials as were used in Germany: coconuts, Rhenish stoneware, Venetian glass, agate, ivory, mother of pearl, rock crystal, with its legendary powers of detecting poison, and imported oriental porcelain, so admired for its superb translucency.

From Germany, too, came the repertoire of northern renaissance ornament: strap-work patterns, animals, flowers, fish, masks and classical urns. Many of the allegorical references are incomprehensible today, but we cannot fail to admire the wealth of detail even if it lacks delicacy.

The standing cup and salt were accorded the richest decoration. They reflect the opulence of an age of great prosperity and confidence, the demand for lavish show of a rising middle class. The displays of wealth demanded by Queen Elizabeth as she progressed through her realm visit-

Left: Design for the Jane Seymour Cup by Hans Holbein (1497/8–1543). (British Museum, London). Right: Design for a jug by Adam van Vianen (1570–1627), Utrecht. Engraved by Theodor van Kessel. (Victoria and Albert Museum, London)

ing her nobility should be remembered. A nobleman would strive to win favour by the grandiose way in which he received and fêted her. No doubt many elaborate pieces of silver would be specially ordered in preparation for a brief visit of this kind.

The dining-table must have presented a magnificent spectacle, set out with tall cups and salts. The ewer and basin also played an important role. Shakespeare mentions their use in 'The Taming of the Shrew', Act II, Scene I:

    Let one attend with silver bason
    Full of rose-water and bestrew'd with flowers,
    Another bear the ewer, the third a diaper.

Glasses were still rare so silver winecups were in general use. The *tazza* and beaker were common pieces, and the tankard, with its tapering body, domed lid and bold S-scroll handle, was a sizeable drinking-vessel. Some flagons took the form of tall tankards.

The same flamboyance was carried on into the reign of James I. The standing cup, however, was heightened by the addition of an obelisk finial. Solid or pierced, this was a specifically English feature reminiscent of contemporary architecture and tomb-ornament. These 'steeples'

were generally raised on scrolled brackets and lent their name to the cups and salts which they adorned.

Gradually, the character of the ornament began to change. More abstract patterns on a larger scale replaced the minute and lively decoration of Elizabethan days. Increasing Dutch influence eclipsed the German, this trend becoming more pronounced in the reign of James' son, Charles I.

The golden years of Dutch silver

Holland had entered into the Renaissance in much the same spirit as Germany in the sixteenth century. The pattern-book had played an important part; imported German books had been in circulation, while in Holland Balthasar Sylvius was producing his own engravings. Mounted pieces appeared in great number, the silver beaker becoming an important Dutch piece.

But now, in the early seventeenth century, Dutch silver rose to international fame. Genre scenes and landscape

Louis XIV visiting the Gobelins factory, one of the tapestries in the series 'The History of the King', woven in the workshop of Jean Jans the Younger (1673–80), after a cartoon by Charles Lebrun. (Mobilier National, Paris)

subjects – so popular with the contemporary artist – were ingeniously transferred to plate. Graduated depths of embossing lent a deceptive sense of depth to the scenes.

It was in Holland that auricular decoration was born, its fleshy, sinuous curves echoing the gristly convolutions of the human ear. The Van Vianen family were responsible for this fashion. Paul van Vianen was silversmith to the Emperor Rudolf II and both he and his brother, Adam, made great use of this bizarre ornament. Adam's son, Christian, took the style to London.

There had been Dutch silversmiths working in London previously – during Elizabeth's reign, several thousand Protestant refugees had emigrated to London from Holland – but Christian van Vianen is the most famous of all. His career is well documented; we know that he arrived in London in 1630 and was soon established in court circles. His most famous work was the altar set made for the Chapel of the Knights of the Order of the Garter, St. George's, Windsor. This was melted down in 1642, but several extant pieces made at this date give a clear idea of his style with its characteristic flowing, auricular patterns. He returned to Utrecht during the Civil War and, in 1650, belatedly published a book of his father's designs called 'Modelles Artificiels'.

Christian van Vianen's work is well known in Holland, and in England he is celebrated for the pieces he made for King Charles at the very time when silver commissions were becoming rare. His extravagant embossing is far removed from the restrained punching of his English colleagues, his bold patterns in marked contrast to their repetitive designs of stylized flowers.

Van Vianen's work is a final extravaganza before a period of artistic arrest. The Civil War broke out in England, culminating in 1649 in the execution of Christian's erstwhile patron, Charles I. For ten years afterwards a Puritan regime held power under the leadership of Oliver Cromwell. The slow process of recuperation – rather than the puritanical tendencies of its governors – may be held responsible for the lack of mid-century plate in England.

But England was not alone. There was a lull over much of Europe during the Thirty Years' War (1618–48) and France suffered during the two Frondes (1648–53). Thus, there was widespread destruction and lack of productivity.

In the late seventeenth century, Holland regained her prosperity and became the trading centre of Europe. She boasted an extremely wealthy middle class and a different social structure from the aristocratic hierarchies of England and France, a difference that is emphasized in the paintings and other works of art commissioned at that time. The well-to-do burgher would certainly buy plate, which would, after all, be a symbol of his prestige, but he would demand a homelier style than that prevalent in England and France.

Holland has always been renowned for her engraving and, in the seventeenth century, flower patterns were the principal decorative motifs. Around 1630 the decorative potential of the tulip was realized and, thereafter, this flower was chiefly depicted. Embossing gained in favour; soon the tulip came to be represented in a riot of foliage which, in its high relief punching and surface-chased

10

details, gained a deceptive realism. Once again there is a link here with painting, for the same *trompe l'œil* flower-subjects are found on canvases of the same date.

One of the most popular collector's pieces today is the Dutch seventeenth-century wager-cup, originally intended for that Dutch spirit, gin. It is often shaped like a full-skirted woman supporting a small bowl upon her head. A swivel mechanism enables wine to be drunk from the large bowl created by her skirt and a strong spirit – brandy or gin – from the smaller cup above. But it requires skill, sobriety and, no doubt, constant practice to carry out this delicate manoeuvre without spilling a drop.

An earthy idea of this kind would never have been countenanced by the refined French who set great store by their table-manners. It bears the unmistakable exuberance of the Dutch people in this flamboyant age of the Baroque.

The baroque style

The new style had emerged in Italy early in the seventeenth century as part of the Counter Reformation. The Jesuits, anxious to draw back their large congregations which had recently been so sadly depleted, commissioned elaborate decorations for their churches. It was hoped that dazzling splendour would attract the impartial onlooker by appealing to his emotions. Marble, gilding, sculpture, *trompe l'œil* painting were all combined in an explosion of irresistible decoration. Confronted today by a baroque church interior, it is still difficult to withstand that forceful theatrical grandeur.

The powerful impact of the style was not lost on the other countries of Europe – indeed, we have seen how Holland was affected by it. Many Catholic nations took their cue from papist Rome and created similar churches. The secular baroque buildings of Rome were also copied. In great Northern palaces, the style was used more as an assertion of power than in dedication to the glory of God. The most famous example of this is, of course, Versailles, created to serve as a dazzling backdrop for the powerful Louis XIV. The psychological impact of the style was used to impress the very countries which were reeling from French political aggression.

Italy had been the artistic leader of Europe for so long, bringing the renaissance and baroque styles to the rest of Europe, but now France was to rise as the instigator of fashion in her stead. Louis' minister, Colbert, strove to build up the arts in France for export reasons. He encouraged great specialization and a rigorous training for all craftsmen. Although the King could grant privileges to favourites, most workmen had to adhere to the stringent regulations of the guilds. The constant supervision of work, the checking of finished products, the insistence upon a high standard, must have harassed workmen and made their task a difficult one, but it had the desired effect. Standards of craftsmanship soared and were kept up until the Revolution in the late eighteenth century.

The furnishings of the royal palaces were produced at the Gobelins factory under the directorship of Charles Lebrun. Lebrun was a great classicist and it was he who was largely responsible for the classical tendencies of French Baroque, so different from the Dutch interpretation of the same style. Some notion of the magnificence of Gobelins plate can be gained from a tapestry depicting Louis XIV visiting the factory. Amid a sea of treasures, workmen are seen staggering under the weight of a colossal silver vase. Many of the furnishings at Versailles were made from solid silver, but they disappeared later in his reign when Louis ordered plate to be melted down. Ironically, the best impression of these silver sets can be gained in England from pieces that were made in imitation of the French originals; several pieces presented to Charles II and William and Mary are at Windsor Castle.

Late seventeenth-century English silver

Charles II was restored to the English throne in 1660 having spent his years of exile in Holland and France. From Holland came the strongest influence on the decorative arts immediately after his return, and English silversmiths aped the florid, floral ornament and deep embossing of ebullient Dutch silver. The standing-cup and salt all but disappeared and the dumpy, two-handled cup, called a 'porringer', 'caudle-cup' or 'posset-cup', appeared as a ceremonial piece in their place.

As social habits changed new pieces made their appearance; it was during these years that coffee- and chocolate-drinking became *de rigueur* and tapering cylindrical pots came into use as containers. Similar in shape to the coffee-pot, the chocolate-pot is distinguishable by the hole set in its lid – generally under a hinged finial – through which a long spoon was passed to whip up the frothy drink.

The same tall, tapering shape was used for the early teapot but, by the 1680s, the low shape, still used today, had been adapted from imported Chinese pottery examples. And with the teapot came all the paraphernalia of tea-making. A few extremely impractical silver tea-bowls were made, and pairs or sets of canisters were provided for storing green and black tea. These were later named '*kati*' (hence 'caddy'), which is a Malayan word for a measure of tea. Chinese ornament was considered appropriate for these pieces and both engravers and chasers took their inspiration from the exotic lacquer, textiles and porcelain which the East India Company was bringing into London.

The Edict of Nantes revoked

Paradoxically, French influence overrode Dutch at the very moment when a Dutch king, William of Orange, came to the English throne. For Europe, already dazzled by Versailles, was further affected by an important political event in France. In 1685 Louis XIV revoked the Edict of Nantes in a bid to enforce Catholicism throughout the land. The freedom of the Huguenot population was thus curtailed and an appalling campaign of persecution was mounted.

In many cases this had the desired effect and large numbers were converted to Catholicism; but many fled abroad. Louis' scandalous intolerance severely damaged his reputation in Europe, while other countries undoubtedly benefited from this influx of French refugees, many of whom had worked as artists or craftsmen before their flight from France.

A threatened section of the community, they had been trained in the rigorous guild manner of the day and had worked hard to justify their existence in their native land. Now, as they arrived in their adoptive countries, they were short of money and eager to find work. Their presence was naturally a threat to the native craftsman, but ultimately he benefited from their greater skill and sense of design. Above all, the French brought new ideas for shapes and decoration, maybe a year or two out of date by Parisian standards – most of them came from the provinces – but still of great interest to foreigners. It was by this means that the French style was disseminated abroad.

In Germany, Holland and England the French version of the Baroque was adopted. The greatest impact would seem to have been upon England, for many of the Huguenots who had fled previously to Holland came on to London in the wake of William of Orange, who became king in 1688. Just such a man was Daniel Marot, who described himself as 'Architecte du Roi', dabbled in garden- and furniture-design and produced the 'Nouveau Livre d'Orfèvrerie'.

In 1697 an Act was passed in England altering the silver 'standard': the alloy content in working silver was lessened in order to prevent 'coin clipping'. There was not enough silver to meet the growing demand and smiths had been forced to melt down coins, or clip silver from them, to supplement the sparse supply. The damage to the economy was considerable and the imposition of the Britannia Standard (which raised the silver content for wrought plate while retaining the old standard for the coinage) was the only means of bringing such practices to an end.

English silversmiths complained bitterly that the 'new' silver, being softer, was more difficult to work, but the immigrants, who had been used to a similar standard at home, adapted to the change with the greatest of ease. This situation gave them the opportunity they sought; they shone beside their English colleagues and by 1720, when the Act was repealed, they were thoroughly at home working in England. Many French names occur in the record of Goldsmiths' Hall, and some of England's most famous eighteenth-century silversmiths are of Huguenot stock, notably Paul de Lamerie.

The French were responsible for shifting the emphasis from embossing to casting in England. Many surviving pieces bear the Italianate masks and strap-work so typical of their style; these were soldered on. Indeed, it was the French who brought cut-card work to perfection in England, superimposing in a sculptural manner layer upon layer of silver. Some cut-card additions were pierced, and piercing reached great delicacy at that time, especially on the lids of casters.

Perhaps the most resplendent French cast work is to be seen in those scrolling figure-handles which appear on the helmet-shaped ewers, popularized in England by the French. They brought not only their own style of decoration but several new pieces to England. The tureen – originally *terrine* – appears to have come from France,

Above: Designs for silver vessels by Daniel Marot (c.1663– 1752), Amsterdam. (Victoria and Albert Museum, London). Above right: Signature of Paul de Lamerie (1688–1751). Right: Design for a tureen by Nicholas Sprimont, c.1750 (Victoria and Albert Museum, London)

while the *écuelle,* with its flat side-handles, had a great popularity in Scotland, where it was known as the 'quaich'.

Early American silver

The fluctuating Dutch and French influences in England were echoed in American work of the same period. New York remained closely linked in style to Holland, even after it had been ceded to England in 1674 and despite the later effects of the Revocation of the Edict of Nantes. Many Dutch smiths were working there, whereas Philadelphia and Boston were more in tune with the British style. Many of the pieces were based upon imported English examples, and there was little time-lag in the adoption of English designs. Daniel Neal wrote of the Bostonians in 1718: 'they affect to be as much English as possible, there is no Fashion in London but three or four months is to be seen here in Boston'.

There was an influx of French Huguenot silversmiths, in the last years of the seventeenth century, who did much to shape the silver fashions of the early seventeen hundreds. As the Queen Anne style developed in England, so the Colonies followed suit. English smiths and engravers worked there and engraved London designs were circulated.

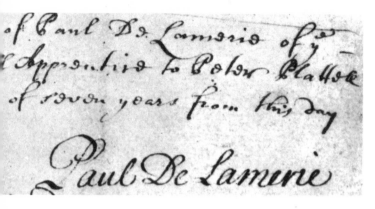

The Queen Anne style

Silver made in the British Isles in the opening years of the eighteenth century relies for its beauty on elegant curved lines and unadorned surfaces. Although the French craftsmen continued to work in a monumental vein, English smiths reduced ornament and simplified form. The bun- or pear-shaped teapot, the salvers, canisters and two-handled cups display this simplicity. Embossing and chasing all but disappeared and frequently the only ornament upon a piece was the heraldic engraving, framed in scrolling arabesque patterns. In an age when both architecture and furniture showed a feeling for perfect proportion and form, silver in its turn reflected a superb awareness of line.

The growth of Rococo

France had gained artistic ascendancy over Italy in the seventeenth century. She fully asserted her independence in the development of a new, specifically French, style: the Rococo. This evolved in the period of the Régence (1715–23), reaching its zenith during the reign of Louis XV. One senses in the frivolity of the new style a conscious reaction to the ponderous grandeur of Louis XIV's reign, as the pattern of life at Versailles changed. An atmosphere of informality and relaxation pervaded the Palace where, only a short time before, a stringently formal code of behaviour had been built up. Madame de Pompadour, who was of the

Parisian bourgeoisie and would therefore never have gained admittance to Court during the previous reign, became the King's mistress and, incidentally, one of the greatest art patrons of her day. The intimate spirit of the age was transmitted to all branches of the arts.

One of the chief instigators of the Rococo was Juste-Aurèle Meissonnier (1695–1730), designer and silversmith. His designs incorporate many of the *rocaille* (rock-work) shapes which were to give the style its name at a later date, used with a disregard for symmetry that was so characteristic of the period. The swirling lines and organic motifs were taken up by the silversmiths of the day, notably Thomas Germain (1673–1748) and his son, François-Thomas Germain (1726–91). The latter went bankrupt in 1765 despite his highly successful practice which extended far beyond the borders of Paris. His work had reached the Courts of Russia and Portugal and was much imitated in these countries. The Rococo spread rapidly, perhaps achieving its most extravagant form in Bavaria, and by the middle of the eighteenth century most of the arts of Europe bear the stamp of this restive French ornament.

In England the Rococo emerged gradually leading by the mid-century to wild extravaganzas of design which tested the skill of even the most experienced craftsmen. Embossing, chasing, engraving, cut-card work and piercing were all combined in lively, inventive designs. One of the silversmiths working in London was the Belgian Nicholas Sprimont, whose work comes closer to *rocaille* than that of his colleagues. After a brief term as goldsmith, however, he transferred his designs to the medium of soft-paste porcelain and started the Chelsea factory.

Undoubtedly the greatest silversmith of the period was a second generation Huguenot, Paul de Lamerie (1688–1751). The quality of his work was at all times superb; the range of his talent is shown by the fact that he was producing plain, undecorated silver at the same time as he was working on his most flamboyant pieces. While many of his colleagues were indulging in wild and unbalanced designs, De Lamerie preserved a wonderful sense of balance and proportion.

One of the most popular shapes of the day was the inverted pear, used for teapots, kettles and canisters. Many of these were decorated with appropriate *chinoiseries* in relief. Salver-rims took on broken patterns and engraving showed a greater richness, the frames of coats of arms echoing the fretted asymmetry of *rocaille*. Piercing on casters, bread-baskets and epergnes also took on irregular patterns and were lavishly decorated. One of the most splendidly pierced pieces was the dish-ring, which was a speciality of Ireland. In Scotland, too, the Rococo was widely adopted. Like Ireland, Scotland followed closely behind England and had its specialities, among them the ring-shaped plaid brooch and heart-brooch, or 'luckenbooth'.

America, likewise, followed suit. The broken outlines and C-scroll ornament were adopted there and the same high standard of craftsmanship was maintained. It was during these years that the famous Boston smith, Paul Revere (1735–1818), was at work.

The Rococo inevitably began to cloy after the middle of the eighteenth century. After so much fussy ornament, there was a preference for simplicity again, and the reaction was

Tureen for Sir Watkin Wynn Baronet

accelerated by a renewed interest in antiquity. Interest in classical architecture and design had never really disappeared since the Renaissance; after all, Classical learning formed the basis of Western education and generations of architects and artists had made pilgrimages to Rome over the years to study at the source of Western Art. But now there was a more fervent attempt to revive Classicism. A flood of publications urged the rejection of the Rococo in favour of a return to the purity of Rome and Greece. A further stimulus was supplied by the excavations at Herculaneum and Pompeii. These towns, sealed by the lava of Vesuvius in 79 A.D. were now uncovered, virtually intact, providing fresh information for the archaeologists.

By the mid-1760s changes were apparent in the arts of Europe, and the United States were soon affected also. Silver reflected the classical trends of the age; the classical column was adapted as a candlestick; the urn was adapted to hold tea, coffee, chocolate or sauces. Fluting, beading, swags of flowers or corn husks were favoured, especially by the engraver, and embossing fell from favour. The clear, unbroken curve of the oval was widely used.

In Britain, the pioneer of the neoclassical revival was the Scottish architect-designer Robert Adam. He collaborated with the metalworker Matthew Boulton, of Soho, Birmingham, who is important not only for his silver but also for drawing attention to the northern centres of Birmingham and Sheffield, which were beginning to rival London in the production of silverware. Sheffield plate (fine sheets of silver fused over a copper core) had already been developed and now gained in importance, bringing cheap silver into the homes of a lowlier clientele.

Another important English silversmith working in the neoclassical taste was Hester Bateman, who took over her husband's business after his death in 1760. Her work, decorated with beading, regular piercing – often set off by glass liners – and bright-cut engraving, displays the characteristic elegance of the day. Bright-cutting has a sparkling quality caused by burnishing as the graver cuts the metal; it appears to have been used in preference to plain engraving by many late eighteenth-century smiths.

In France, silver followed much the same pattern in these final years of royal patronage prior to the Revolution and the disintegration of the guilds. One particular branch of

14

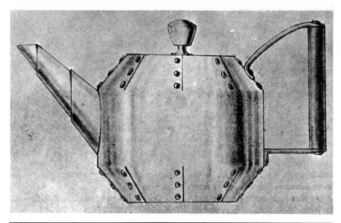

Left: Design for a tureen by Robert Adam, 1773. (Sir John Soane Museum, London) Above: Design for a teapot by Christopher Dresser, c.1899 for Messrs. Elkington & Co. (Private Collection) Below: Electroplated nickel silver teapot by Christopher Dresser, 1880. Made by James Dixon and Sons. (Victoria and Albert Museum, London)

French *orfèvrerie*, the manufacture of gold and silver boxes, reached its zenith at that time.

Little boxes for snuff, rouge or patches had been made in the seventeenth century. As the eighteenth century progressed they increased in popularity, especially after they became accepted at court as a means of bestowing favour. Often encrusted with valuable jewels, it was understood that the recipient would probably 'cash in' his gift: it was merely a tactful and attractive way of handing over a sum of money. In Meissonnier's day, elaborate chasing had been used; later, enamelling grew more fashionable. Several shades of gold were sometimes used in conjunction on a box and, in Louis XIV's reign, exotic materials were mounted: mother of pearl, painted ivory, onyx, tortoise-shell, Sèvres plaques and Japanese lacquer. Napoleon continued to use boxes as gifts in the next century although, with the breakdown of guild control and the gradual decrease of skilled craftsmen, this luxury product was naturally to suffer.

The neoclassical revival extended well into the nineteenth century. In silver the slender elegance of the 1780s and '90s gave way to a sculptural monumentality, as the light-hearted interpretation of Classicism was replaced by a more serious evocation of the past. This craving for exactitude – so typical of the century – seemed often to lead to stiff and lifeless design.

The grandeur of Napoleon's plate, as made by such smiths as Auguste, Biennais and Odiot, found an echo in much European work. Meanwhile a similar path was followed in England by Paul Storr and his colleagues at the firm of Rundell, Bridge and Rundell: formal candlesticks and careful reproductions of classical urns emerged from the workshops of both countries. Many were ordered to commemorate the various victories of the Napoleonic wars; the Nile campaign is recollected in Egyptian motifs such as the lotus flower. Indeed, it was the French who were responsible for stimulating interest in that little-known ancient civilization.

The 'battle of the styles'

The eclecticism of the early decades of the nineteenth century foreshadows many later developments. The industrial advance of Europe had progressed at such a rate that there was an inevitable reaction. Designers – apparently incapable of facing up to modern technology and the scope it offered – took shelter in the past, and Europe was swept by revival after revival. Classicism sustained a long popularity; the Rococo was reborn; the Renaissance and the Baroque appear incongruously side by side. A designer would often select a style from this wide choice for its associations. Thus the Gothic, revived by Viollet-le-Duc in France and Pugin and Burges in England, was considered especially apt for ecclesiastical plate, evoking a suitably medieval, Christian atmosphere.

A complete *mêlée* of styles was displayed in the mid-century exhibitions. One important characteristic prevailed: plate in the rococo, renaissance, gothic, *chinoiserie* and baroque styles all evince a passion for extravagant ornament. No wonder the elaborate chased work of Froment-Meurice and Antoine Vechte won them such international acclaim in their day. Very few people can have agreed with the English designer Christopher Dresser when he wrote: 'Silver and gold being materials of considerable worth, it is necessary that the utmost economy be observed is using them'. There were those, especially towards the end of the century, who fought against the dire effects of mass production. Men such as William Morris, in urging a return to craftsmanship, were advocating escapism, too, although they turned to the past not so much for stylistic inspiration but for technique. Nonetheless, their determination to keep old crafts alive was successful and from them stems the independent artist-craftsman of the present century. However, not even the opinions they expressed could prevent the general mechanization of an ancient art.

Towards the turn of the century a new style emerged, concurrently in Europe and America: Art Nouveau. Its elongated proportions and elegant swirling lines are original and, at last, the dependence on past style subsided. The plainer shapes of much twentieth-century plate bear this out and show an understanding of the potential of our modern age. Silversmithing is still maintaining its place in the applied arts despite competition from new materials.

Glossary of terms

Champlevé. Grooves or troughs are cut into the metal to be decorated, and these are filled with enamel ingredients which are then fused and polished.

Chasing. Decorating metal by hammering from the front of the object; also the finishing process of chiselling cast metal.

Cloisonné. One of the oldest methods of enamelling. A network of metal cells is soldered to the surface of the object and the enamels are poured into these enclosures. The network of wire is still visible and forms borders round the different colours.

Cut-card work. Flat sheet-metal cut into shapes and soldered on to the object to be decorated. Much used by the Huguenots.

Embossing. Decorating metal by hammering from the back of the object.

Engraving. The method of inscribing or ornamenting metal with a cutting-tool, producing a thin line. Bright-cut engraving is the process of engraving with an angled tool, thereby removing part of the metal and leaving a faceted surface.

Festoon. Garland of leaves or flowers hanging in a curve.

Fluting. Channelled decoration used vertically or obliquely.

Gadrooning. Relief ornament of parallel convex ribs used vertically or obliquely; the reverse of fluting.

Gilding. Before about 1840 the usual method of gilding metal was to mix the gold with mercury, apply it to the metal object and heat it. In this way the mercury evaporated and the gold remained on the object in a thin layer. With the invention of electro-plating the mercury process was largely abandoned. Parcel-gilt is the term used to describe an article of which only part has been gilded. Silver-gilt refers to a silver object, gilt either to prevent tarnishing or to give a richer appearance. The inside of silver salt-cellars were sometimes gilt before the introduction of glass liners, to prevent damage caused by the contact of salt with silver.

Grotesque. A form of ornament which became known at the end of the fifteenth century on the discovery of wall-paintings in houses being excavated in Rome. The shapes are based on human, plant and animal forms and were published as engravings at the beginning of the sixteenth century, immediately becoming popular with craftsmen and ornamentalists.

Lambrequin. Draped and tasselled border decoration.

Lobing. Gadrooning.

Niello. A black alloy of sulphur, lead, silver and copper used to fill engraved decoration on silver, then heated and the excess rubbed away, leaving a contrasting inlay.

Punched work. A decorative treatment of metal done by embossing it with blunt tools used in groups to form a design of flowers or geometrical shapes. Mainly used in the seventeenth century.

Bibliography

Banister, J., *An Introduction to Old English Silver*, Evans, London 1965

Davis, F., *French Silver 1450–1825*, Arthur Barker, London 1970

Hayward, J. F., *Huguenot Silver in England 1688–1727*, Faber and Faber, London 1959

Phillips, J. M., *American Silver*, American Craft Series, New York 1949

Rowe, R., *Adam Silver*, Faber and Faber, London 1965

Taylor, G., *Continental Gold and Silver*, The Connoisseur and Michael Joseph, London 1967

Taylor, G., *Silver*, Penguin Books, Harmondsworth 1956; revised ed. Pelican, Baltimore 1964

Wardle, P., *Victorian Silver and Silver Plate*, Herbert Jenkins, London 1963; Universe Books, New York 1970

Acknowledgments

Art Gallery and Museum, Glasgow: 27. Ashmolean Museum, Oxford: 23, 34, 45. Museum of Fine Arts, Boston, Massachusetts: 71. BPC Publishing Ltd., London: 3, 4, 6, 7, 8, 9, 10, 11, 12 14, 17, 22, 25, 28, 29, 31, 33, 38, 39, 43, 46, 47, 48, 49, 50, 51, 52, 53, 54, 55, 57, 58, 59, 60, 61, 62, 63, 64, 66, 67, 74, 75, 76, 77, 79, 80, 83, 84, 85, 86, 87, 88, 89. Calouste Gulbenkian Foundation, Lisbon: 41, 42. Christie, Manson and Woods Ltd., London: 26. City of Manchester Art Gallery: 37. Cooper-Bridgeman Library: 65. Fitzwilliam Museum, Cambridge: 56. Fratelli Fabbri: 30. J. Freeman: 2, 21. M. Gerson: 35. Giraudon, Paris: 40. London Museum: 18. Musée des Arts Decoratifs, Paris: 44. P. Parkinson: 16, 19, 20, 24, 32, 36, 78, 81, 82. Rijksmuseum, Amsterdam: 13. Scala, Milan: 5. J. Szaezfai: 68, 69, 70, 72, 73. Trinity College, Oxford: 15. Victoria and Albert Museum, London: 1.

1 *The Burghley Nef* by Pierre le Flamand, French. 1482–83. (Victoria and Albert Museum, London.) In medieval times the nef – a decorative and highly elaborate model of a ship – was used in many countries in the same way as the ceremonial salt in England. Nefs – including this example – were often also salt-cellars but their chief function was to mark the position occupied by the most important diner. This nef uses a nautilus shell for the hull of the ship, which is supported on the back of a mermaid. The remainder of the ship is of silver, parcel-gilt. The figures of Tristram and Isolde are seated in front of the main mast, playing a game of chess. The nef was for some years in the possession of the Exeters at Burghley House, Lincolnshire, from where it takes its name.

2 *Casket*, Spanish. *c.*1640. (Victoria and Albert Museum, London.) This casket was probably used to hold corporals – the cloths on which consecrated elements are placed during the celebration of mass. It is made of silver and gilt bronze and is lined with red damask which has a silk panel embroidered with flowers and the inscription IHS in gold thread. The embossed strap-work and the feet in the form of cherubs are characteristic motifs of the period. Church plate was of far greater importance than secular plate in Catholic Spain. Commissioned in lavish manner by the clergy or the devout nobility, the treasures of Spain are the richest in Europe.

3 *Ewer and basin*, Spanish, from Aragon or Castile. Late sixteenth century. (Victoria and Albert Museum, London.) Ewer and basin sets were intended for washing the hands. They were for both ecclesiastical and secular use and were among the most important pieces of early plate. It would appear that this very fine set was made for a private house, since it bears a coat of arms. It is in silver, parcel-gilt, the gilding having been applied to certain areas to emphasize the decoration. The firmly articulated decoration on the rim of the ewer accords well with the substantial appearance of the objects owing to the quantity of metal employed. These are characteristics of Spanish plate.

4 *The Schlüsselfelder Nef*, possibly by Hans Krug, Nuremberg. *c.*1503. (German-isches Nationalmuseum, Nuremberg. Lent by the Schlüsselfelder family.) This centrepiece, which bears the Nuremberg mark, was at one time thought to be the work of Albrecht Dürer the Elder, father of the famous artist. It is an exceptionally fine and accurate representation of a particular contemporary ship. The influence of the Renaissance can be seen in the supporting mermaid figure.

5 *Covered goblet* by Friedrich Hillebrandt (d.1608), Nuremberg. 1595. (German-isches Nationalmuseum, Nuremberg.) The most distinguished member of a family of Nuremberg goldsmiths, Friedrich Hillebrandt specialized in the setting of nautilus shells in elaborate silver mounts. This is one of his most remarkable surviving pieces, superbly executed with fine mannerist detail. The nautilus shell is supported by a straining figure of Atlas, and the cover is surmounted by Neptune and winged horses.

6

6 *Salt-cellar*, Augsburg. Late seventeenth century. (Victoria and Albert Museum, London.) It was fashionable during the seventeenth century to make drinking-vessels and other such pieces in the form of animals. This salt-cellar, which is seven and a half inches high, is modelled as a monster, holding a scallop shell in its claws.

7 *Salt*, Nuremberg. 1550. (S. J. Phillips, Ltd., London.) This silver salt is decorated with gilt medallions in the manner of Peter Flötner, an influential sculptor at the time of the German Renaissance.

8 *Beaker* by Christian Metz, Ohlau. Late seventeenth century. (Victoria and Albert Museum, London.) This small beaker – it is only four and a half inches high – is lavishly engraved with flowers and parcel gilt.

7

8

9 *Beaker and cover*, maker's mark $\frac{SB}{F}$, Augsburg. Late seventeenth century. (Victoria and Albert Museum, London.) This silver-gilt drinking-cup is ornamented with embossed and chased flowers.

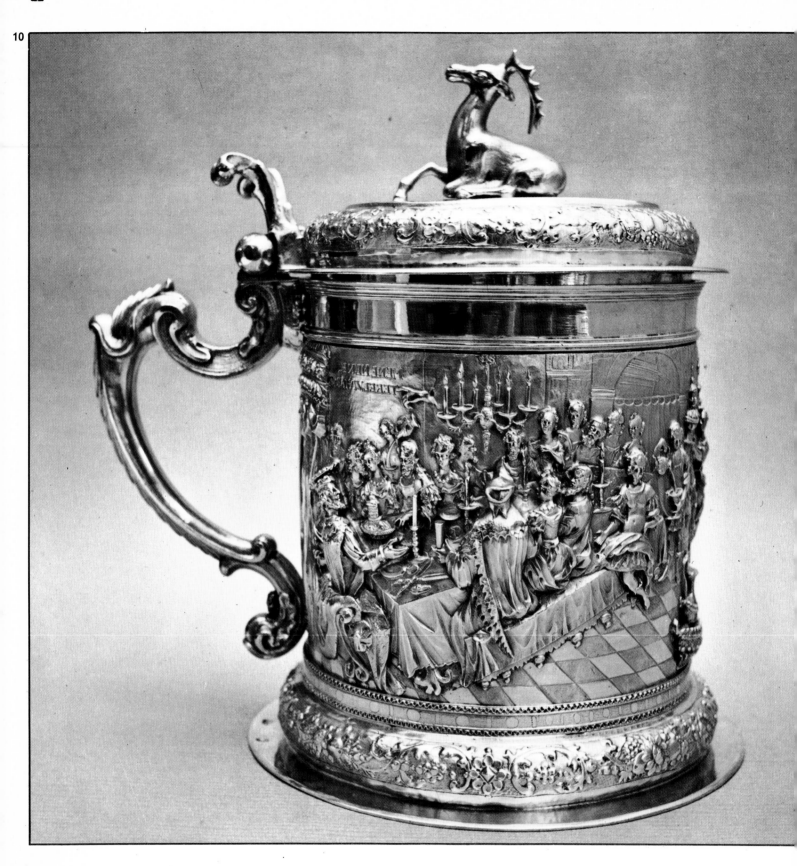

10 *Tankard* by Daniel Mylius, Danzig. *c.*1700. (Victoria and Albert Museum, London.) This magnificent piece is of silver-gilt and decorated with an embossed Biblical scene. Drinking-vessels form the major part of German silver of this period and there was a strong tendency to lavishness in ornamental detail.

11 *Standing cup and cover*, German. Eighteenth century. (Victoria and Albert Museum, London.) This silver-gilt cup shows the unusual combination of horn and mother of pearl; the panels of the latter material are finely engraved with hunting scenes.

1

12 *Beaker and cover* by Johann Erhard Henglin, Augsburg. *c.*1720. (Victoria and Albert Museum, London.) This beaker shows a form of decoration popular in Germany at the beginning of the eighteenth century, known as *Laub und Bandelwerk* (foliage and scroll-work).

12

14

13

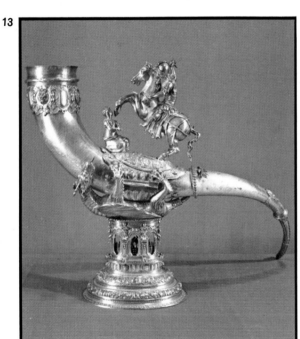

13 *Drinking-horn* of the Guild of St George, Amsterdam. 1566. (Rijksmuseum, Amsterdam.) In the form of a medieval drinking-horn, this vessel has a circular base chased with bands of fruit and other ornamental devices; the stem bears cherubs' heads and female terms rising to a supine dragon which holds the cup. The silver horn is surmounted by the figure of St George mounted on a rearing horse.

14 *Clock*, the movement by Adriaen van den Bergh, the case by Hans Conraedt Breghtel, The Hague. *c.*1600. (Victoria and Albert Museum, London.) This magnificent Dutch clock is very similar to German designs in its decorative motifs. The compressed ball feet, however, are a distinctively Dutch feature originally borrowed from Spain and much used on furniture of the period.

15 *Standing salt*, maker's mark a swan's head erased, London. 1549. (Trinity College, Oxford.) From medieval days until the seventeenth century the salt was an important feature of the table and was in size and ornament the object of lavish display. A number of fine ceremonial salts were made of rock crystal. This example encloses a standing figure within the column and is mounted with scrolled caryatids and other embellishments of silver-gilt.

16 *Standing cup*, London. 1545. (The Worshipful Company of Goldsmiths, London.) The bowl of this cup, which is held between the foot and the cup-shaped engraved lip by three slender straps, is of faceted rock crystal.

17 *Ewer*. Sixteenth or early seventeenth century. (Victoria and Albert Museum, London.) This ewer was made in China during the Ming period (1368–1644) and brought to England, where it was finished with silver-gilt mounts. This was not an uncommon occurrence, but English silversmiths unfortunately made little or no effort to produce mounts for Oriental porcelain in anything but the current European style; consequently such pieces have rather an incongruous effect.

18 *The Sudeley Tankard*, also known as the Parr Pot, the silver-gilt mounts with maker's mark a fleur de lis and hall-marked for 1546. London. (London Museum, London.) The cover is enamelled with the arms of Sir William Parr, uncle of Katharine Parr, sixth wife of Henry VIII. He was also chamberlain to Elizabeth I; the piece was probably presented to him by the Queen. The body is of striated milk glass, or *latticinio*, imported from Venice. The tankard is one of the finest early English mounted-glass pieces to survive and, glass being rare at this date, it would have been greatly valued by its original owner.

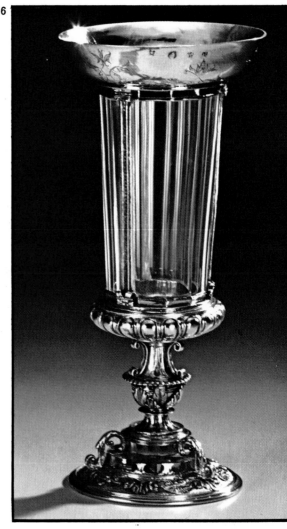

16

18

19   *The Bowes Cup*, London. 1554. (The Worshipful Company of Goldsmiths, London.) The original owner of this cup was Sir Martin Bowes, Prime Warden of the Goldsmiths, and it was he who presented it to the Company in 1561. It is of silver-gilt with a bowl of crystal.

20   *The Rogers Salt*, London. 1601. (The Worshipful Company of Goldsmiths, London.) This is one of the last great Tudor mounted salts to be made. The cylinder of crystal contains a parchment roll painted with flowers, the arms of the Goldsmiths' Company and an escutcheon inscribed 'Ric. Rogers, Comptroller of the Mint'. The restrained, simple setting is of silver-gilt chased in low relief with a design of formal foliage; the cover is surmounted by a small crystal and a silver steeple.

21   *The Gibbon Salt*, maker's mark three trefoils in a trefoil, London. 1576. (The Worshipful Company of Goldsmiths, London.) The five-sided pillar of rock crystal in the centre of this magnificent piece encloses a figure of Neptune, holding above his head the tiny container for the salt. The silver-gilt framework is architectural in form. The salt is believed to have been given to the Goldsmiths as a bribe to pass substandard silver. An inscription reads: 'The guift of Simon Gibbon Goldsmith 1632'.

22   *The Lambard Cup*, probably made by John Bird, London. 1578. (The Worshipful Company of Drapers, London.) This superb cup was presented to the Drapers' Company on 4 August, 1578, by Mr. William Lambard. It bears the arms of England, those of the Company, and those of Sir William Cordell, Master of the Rolls. The inscription reads: 'A Proctour for the Poore am I & remember theim before thow Dye. 1578'.

23

24

25

26

27

28

23 *Spice-box*, maker's mark II or TI and a mullet, London. 1620. (Ashmolean Museum, Oxford.) The scallop-shell shape was used for spice-boxes from the time of their introduction in the late sixteenth century. Spices brought from overseas were used ever more frequently and these small boxes, their interiors usually divided in half and often containing a spoon, became fashionable in the 1620s.

24 *Grace-cup*, maker's mark RP, London. 1619. (Worshipful Company of Goldsmiths, London.) Many such standing wine-cups were made in this period. The foot was usually circular rising to a slender baluster stem, sometimes, as here, connected to the bowl with small scrolling cast brackets.

25 *Brush*, London. 1683. (Victoria and Albert Museum, London.) Forming part of a toilet-set, this octagonal brush is engraved with Chinese motifs in the current fashion.

26 *Inkstand*, maker's or sponsor's mark AI (probably that of Alexander Jackson), London. 1639. (Christie, Manson and Woods Ltd., London.) This inkstand in the manner of Van Vianen is the finest and largest seventeenth-century example known to exist. The entire surface is enriched with repoussé scroll-work in the auricular style. It is ten and a quarter inches high and sixteen and a half inches wide and has two candle-holders and numerous compartments to hold ink, sand and all the appurtenances of letter-writing at that time.

27 *Set of three steeple-cups*, maker's mark MM TB in monogram, London. 1611–12. (Art Gallery and Museum, Glasgow. Burrell Collection.) Steeple-cups, made from 1599 until about 1646, were a form of cup apparently made only in England, and about one hundred and fifty examples are recorded. The chased ornament varies from foliage and strap-work to shells, animals and fruit.

28 *Salver*, London. c.1685. (Christie, Manson and Woods Ltd., London.) Although very little silver came to Europe from the East, European craftsmen used oriental motifs to decorate their wares, gaining inspiration from imported porcelain and lacquered articles and from contemporary travel-books. The flat surface of a salver provided the ideal opportunity for the engraver to display his skill.

29 *Teapot*, Chinese. 1680s. (Victoria and Albert Museum, London.) This rare, silver-gilt teapot was made in China specifically for the European market. The six panels are decorated with animals and rustic scenes and the spout is in imitation bamboo.

30 *Ewer* by David Willaume, London. 1700. (Victoria and Albert Museum, London.) This is a particularly fine example of the helmet shape introduced to England by the Huguenots at the end of the seventeenth century, after the revocation of the Edict of Nantes in 1685 caused their mass flight from France. The cast detail of this silver-gilt ewer is of exquisite quality, and this is emphasized by the comparatively small scale – the piece is eight and a half inches high. The style of this cast and fluted base was fashionable until the end of the first decade of the eighteenth century.

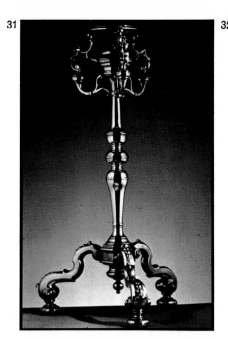

31 *Stand for a tea-kettle*, unmarked, English. *c.*1725. (Victoria and Albert Museum, London.) Tea-kettle stands were made from the end of the seventeenth century and were usually only a few inches in height, since they were intended to stand on a table. In a few rare cases, such as this, the stand itself was formed as a tripod table and made of solid silver.

32 *Tea-canister* by Nathaniel Roe, London. 1713. (Worshipful Company of Goldsmiths, London.) The early form of the tea-canister – not called a caddy until later in the eighteenth century – was similar to that of the Chinese porcelain examples, being rectangular or octagonal. The canister illustrated here is of a slightly later type but the octagonal form persists.

33 *Two tankards*, that on the left by Timbrell and Bentley of London. 1713. That on the right by Nathaniel Locke of London. 1716. (Private Collection.) First made in as early as the fourteenth century, silver tankards were produced in many sizes and variations in ornamental detail. The two illustrated here are typical of those made in the early years of the eighteenth century.

34 *Two-handled* cup by Pierre Platel (*d.*1719), London. 1705. (Ashmolean Museum, Oxford.) A characteristic form of Huguenot decoration was the strap, applied to the lower part of the body and radiating from the base. This was often, as in this example, reinforced by a cast spine to emphasize its sculptural character. The two-handled cup and cover was a popular piece throughout the eighteenth century.

35 *Tea-canister*, probably by Isaac Liger, London. *c.*1706. (Victoria and Albert Museum, London.) Early tea-canisters such as this one, in silver-gilt, usually had a cap cover suitable for use as a measure while making or mixing tea.

36 *Teapot, kettle and chocolate-pot* by Joseph Ward, London. 1719. (Worshipful Company of Goldsmiths, London.) From early in the reign of Queen Anne, silver teapots began to be made in comparatively large numbers, after appearing only rarely in the reign of Charles II. In well-to-do households they were accompanied by large silver kettles with swing handles, mounted on their own matching stands with a spirit-lamp to heat the water. This is an exceptionally fine set including a chocolate-pot, which like the teapot, has its own matching stand. The octagonal pear-shape was typical of this period, fitted with high, domed lids such as these.

37 *Hot-water jug* by Simon Pantin, London. 1712. (City of Manchester Art Galleries. Assheton Bennett Collection.) Simple, well-proportioned pieces were much in vogue during the reigns of Queen Anne and George I. Many of these pieces were made by Huguenots who had fashioned similar pieces for their middle-class French customers. The Huguenot style became identified with fine quality English silver.

38 *Tankard* by Robert Timbrell and Benjamin Bentley, London. 1714–15. (Victoria and Albert Museum, London.) Most tankards of the early eighteenth century held about two pints and involved the use of a great deal of silver. Despite the increased cost resulting from the imposition of the Britannia standard, there was no apparent diminution in the demand. Makers had begun to produce tankards which were slightly narrower and taller but retained the same general outline. One modification around the turn of the century was in the lid; whereas before lids had been flat, or nearly flat, they now developed a low, domed shape, as illustrated by this example.

39 *Chocolate-pot*, maker unknown, London. 1722–23. (Victoria and Albert Museum, London.) Chocolate was introduced into England in the middle of the seventeenth century and was an expensive, and therefore fashionable, drink. No pot specifically made for chocolate is known before 1685 but they were quite common by the early years of the eighteenth century. Chocolate-pots are distinguishable from coffee-pots only in that they incorporate a small aperture in the lid, covered by a hinged or sliding finial, through which the chocolate could be stirred with a special rod.

39

40 *Ecuelle*, Bordeaux. 1744. (Musée des Arts Décoratifs, Paris.) This fine example of French provincial workmanship has traditional features seen on *écuelles* from early in the eighteenth century. Dishes of this sort were in common use throughout France as soup-bowls, but few are known elsewhere. Those made in England were probably introduced by Huguenot craftsmen for their aristocratic clients with continental tastes.

41 *Triple centrepiece for a table* by François-Thomas Germain (*d.*1791). French. 1763–64. (Calouste Gulbenkian Foundation, Lisbon.) A large quantity of French silver which had been made by Thomas Germain (1673–1748) for the Portuguese Court was destroyed by the Lisbon earthquake of 1755, and his son, François-Thomas Germain, was commissioned to provide a number of replacements. This superb three-piece table-centre is one example. It shows laughing, playful *amorini* fighting over plentiful bunches of grapes scattered over a rocky ground on a scrolling, rococo base.

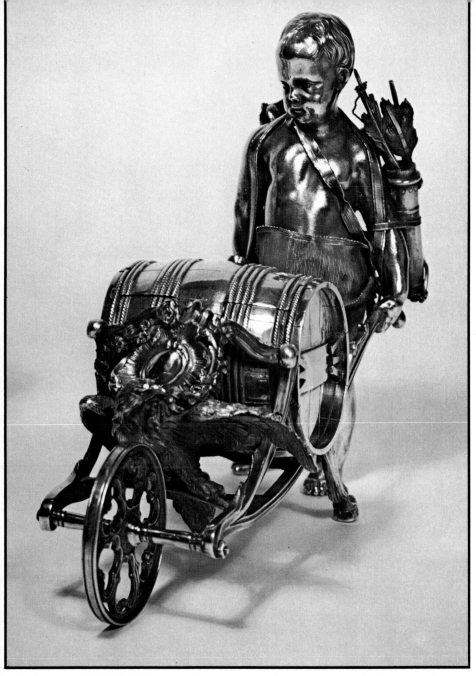

44

42 *Mustard-barrel*, one of a pair by Antoine-Sébastian Durand, Paris. 1750–51. (Calouste Gulbenkian Foundation, Lisbon.) Made for Madame de Pompadour, these mustard-barrels are held on wheelbarrows pushed by a pair of Cupids. A shield-bearing eagle is outspread over each wheel.

43 *Sauce-boat* by François Joubert, Paris. 1754–55. (Musée des Arts Décoratifs, Paris.) In the height of rococo fashion, this richly decorated sauce-boat was also made for the table of Madame de Pompadour and bears her arms. It is of silver, parcel-gilt.

44 *Three-branched candelabrum* by Claude Duvivier, Paris. 1734–35. (Musée des Arts Décoratifs, Paris.) The instigator of the rococo style, with its asymmetrical, swirling lines and fluid, graceful curves was Juste-Aurèle Meissonnier. This candlestick is the execution of one of his many designs for tableware and domestic articles, dating from the 1720s.

45

46

47

48

49

45 *Set of four trencher salts and spoons* by Paul de Lamerie (1688–1751), London. 1727. (Ashmolean Museum, Oxford.) Paul de Lamerie is among the most celebrated of English goldsmiths. Of Huguenot stock, he was apprenticed in 1703 to another Huguenot, the London goldsmith Pierre Platel. Although best known for his elaborate decoration and flamboyant style, De Lamerie also made much simpler pieces, like these salts, which rely solely on their perfection of line and proportion. The interiors of these salts are gilt.

46 *Pierced basket* by Paul de Lamerie, London. 1747. (Ashmolean Museum, Oxford.) The scallop-shell shape was often used by Paul de Lamerie for his tableware. This piece, which is fourteen inches in length, was probably intended for use as a bread-basket; other, smaller shells were made to contain salt. In conjunction with shells, use was often made of other marine motifs such as fish, nets and, as in this case, dolphins. Delicate pierced work was also a speciality of De Lamerie.

47 *Pair of tea-canisters*, unmarked, London. c.1720. (Victoria and Albert Museum, London.) These silver-gilt tea-canisters are thought to be the work of Paul de Lamerie, and the engraving is by Hogarth. They are further examples of De Lamerie's simpler style, and show his minute attention to detail. William Hogarth was apprenticed in 1712 to the goldsmith Ellis Gamble, and there learnt the skills of engraving, which he later applied almost solely to printing and very rarely to silver.

48 *Sugar-caster* by Paul de Lamerie, London. 1734–35. (Victoria and Albert Museum, London.) De Lamerie was one of the first to use the exaggerated and highly ornamental rococo style in England, and this sugar-caster is an early example of the influence on De Lamerie of Juste-Aurèle Meissonnier who was made master of the Paris Goldsmiths' Guild in 1725 and produced many designs for silverware.

49 *Cup and cover* by Paul de Lamerie, London. 1723. (Ashmolean Museum, Oxford.) Fairly restrained in its decoration, this cup follows the fashion for elaborate silver which continued throughout the eighteenth century. The proportions are faultless and the decoration is typical of De Lamerie's superb technical skill.

50 *The Newdigate Centrepiece* by Paul de Lamerie, London. 1743. (Victoria and Albert Museum, London.) This piece is one of the finest examples of rococo work. It can be set up in two ways: either with the four small waiters as shown here, or without them, their places being filled by four ornamental knobs. The centrepiece was made as a wedding gift for Sir Roger and Lady Newdigate from her grandmother, Lady Lempster. It was in this year, 1743, that Paul de Lamerie became Fourth Warden of the Goldsmiths' Company.

51 *Double-branched candlestick*, one of a pair by Frederick Kandler, London. 1752. (Ashmolean Museum, Oxford.) Candlesticks with figure stems appeared towards the end of the seventeenth century; the figures stand or kneel and are usually on a triangular base. These candlesticks retain the triangular base but soften it with strong, sweeping, rococo scrolls and flowers. The elegant female figure supports a two-branched candle-holder surmounted by a flower.

52 *Cup and cover* by William Kidney, London. 1740. (Worshipful Company of Goldsmiths, London.) The two-handled cup and cover appeared in England during the six-teenth century and developed through many different forms. During the eighteenth century it became large and ornate and increasingly an item for use on ceremonial occasions. This magnificent silver-gilt example illustrates perfectly the dramatic effect of surface variations such as matting and burnishing. The sunken matted panel is set off by the plain, burnished background and itself serves as a foil to the raised and burnished central cartouche. The Bacchanalian theme of grapes and drinking figures and the knop in the form of a bust of Silenus point to the intended use of this ceremonial cup.

53 *Sauce-boat*, one of a pair by Charles Kandler, London. 1737. (Ashmolean Museum, Oxford.) Sauce-boats were intro-duced during the reign of George I and were at first double-lipped, with a handle at each side. This form persisted until the 1730s, when they took on the form of a shallow, wide jug, usually with a scroll handle. The shell form naturally suggested itself as an ideal shape and it is probable that sauce-boats such as this, decorated with crabs and having a crane as its handle, were intended to contain sauces for fish.

51

52

53

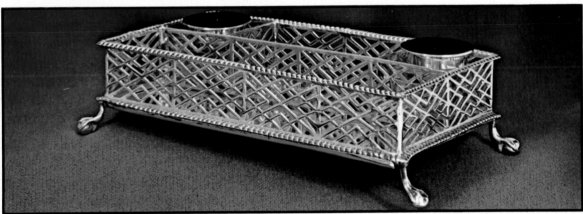

54 *Pair of tea-caddies* by Samuel Courtauld, London. 1760s. (Victoria and Albert Museum, London.) In the middle of the eighteenth century the fashion for *chinoiserie* once more swept England and surfaces of silver objects were covered with delightful and brilliantly modelled repoussé figures and Chinese motifs. Tea-caddies in particular came in for such treatment. This pair is by a member of the Courtauld family of Huguenot goldsmiths who settled in London after the religious restrictions imposed in France at the end of the seventeenth century.

55 *Inkstand*, maker's mark illegible, English. 1759–60. (Private Collection.) Another form of *chinoiserie*, the pattern of this fine and delicate piece is based on fretwork seen on wallpapers, in gardens, and in the recently published furniture-designs of Thomas Chippendale.

56 *Mustard-pot*, English. 1750s. (Fitzwilliam Museum, Cambridge.) It was generally the fashion, until the mid-eighteenth century, for mustard to be brought to the table in its dry state, thus requiring containers similar to sugar-casters. In the 1740s, however, it became customary for mustard already mixed with water to be put on the table, and it was then that the mustard-pot as we now know it became popular, though earlier examples are known. Pierced decoration was fashionable and the pot was usually fitted with a blue glass lining. The example illustrated here displays an elegant and advanced form of *chinoiserie* decoration.

57

57 *Tankard* by Robert Goble, Cork. *c.*1695. (National Museum of Ireland, Dublin.) The maker of this piece was one of Ireland's finest silversmiths. It is partly due to him that his home town of Cork became synonymous with the highest quality in Irish silver. He made many pieces of silver for domestic use, of which a large number survived, and is probably best known as the maker of the mace of the trade guilds of Cork. He died in 1719.

58 *Casters* by David King, Dublin. 1699. (National Museum of Ireland, Dublin.) An early example of the sets of three casters, probably for sugar, pepper and mustard. More generally made in the early eighteenth century, these 'lighthouse' casters are elaborately ornamented with fluting, gadrooning and engraving.

58

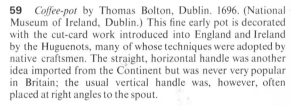

59 *Coffee-pot* by Thomas Bolton, Dublin. 1696. (National Museum of Ireland, Dublin.) This fine early pot is decorated with the cut-card work introduced into England and Ireland by the Huguenots, many of whose techniques were adopted by native craftsmen. The straight, horizontal handle was another idea imported from the Continent but was never very popular in Britain; the usual vertical handle was, however, often placed at right angles to the spout.

60 *Cake-basket* by John Lloyd, Dublin. 1772. (National Museum of Ireland, Dublin.) Silverware made in Ireland was often simpler and less sophisticated than that made in England. This delicate open-work basket is a good example. Many baskets were made in the eighteenth century for use as bread-, cake- or dessert-baskets, and it is known that similar ones were also used to hold sewing materials.

61 *Pair of sauce-boats* by Robert Calderwood, Dublin. *c.*1737. (National Museum of Ireland, Dublin.) Irish sauce-boats followed the same fashion as those made in England. Robert Calderwood made many pieces of good quality domestic silver including some fine candlesticks, dinner-plates and bowls.

62 *Three dish-rings* by John Lloyd, Dublin. 1770–80. (National Museum of Ireland, Dublin.) A typically Irish piece, the dish-ring made its appearance after the middle of the eighteenth century and reached the height of its popularity in the 'seventies. Dish-rings were intended originally to hold hot punch-bowls and later became used to keep any hot dishes off a polished table. They provided a perfect outlet for the inventive skills of the Irish craftsmen, and the delicate pierced decoration of birds, fruit, flowers and pastoral scenes against a foliate or trellis-work background make these dish-rings perhaps the most interesting and delightful examples of Irish silver. They were rarely made elsewhere.

63 *Sauce-boat* by Thomas Walker, Dublin. *c.*1738. (National Museum of Ireland, Dublin.) Made in an extravagant and highly decorative style, this sauce-boat is a particularly fine example of Irish rococo silver. Such elaborate ornament could well make the piece appear heavy but the curve of the rim and the upward sweep of the figure handle contrive to lighten its appearance.

61

62

63

64

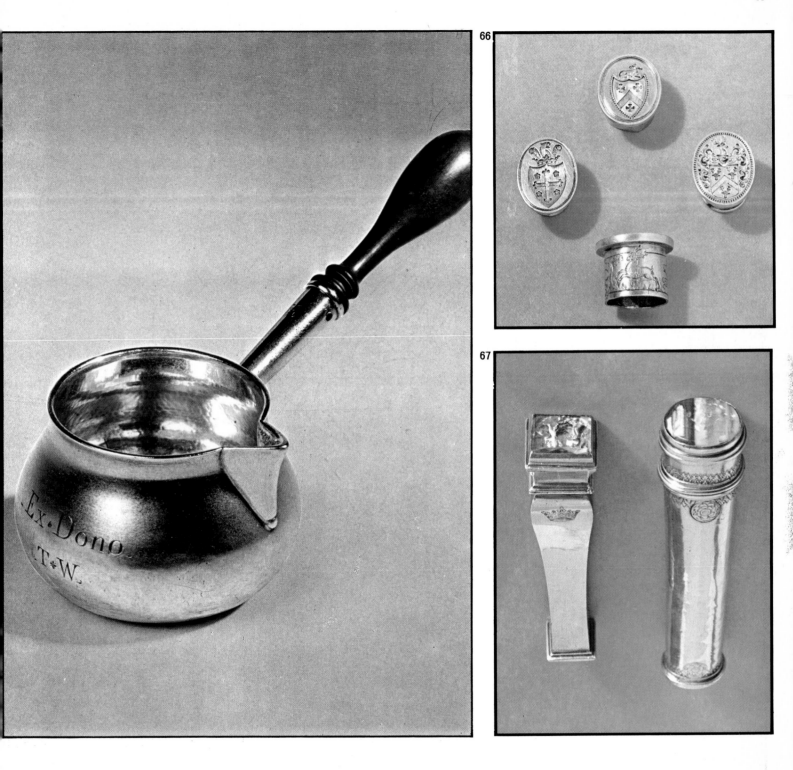

64 *Monteith* by Thomas Bolton, Dublin. *c.*1704. (National Museum of Ireland, Dublin.) The monteith was a large bowl with a notched brim, in which wineglasses were placed to cool, their bowls resting in cold water. They were also used as punch-bowls and the notched rims were often detachable. They were made in England until about 1760 but only a few Irish examples are known. This monteith in silver-gilt is a magnificent specimen of the work of Thomas Bolton.

65 *Saucepan* by William Fleming, English. 1726. (Thomas Lumley, London.) Many examples of these small saucepans survive, and it is thought that they were used for heating brandy. They were made throughout the eighteenth century and were normally devoid of decoration other than, perhaps, an engraved inscription or the coat of arms of their owners. However a few very elaborate examples were made.

66 *Four desk seals*, English. The seals at top and bottom of the illustration are silver seals of the late seventeenth century; those to the left and right are of the second half of the eighteenth century. (Victoria and Albert Museum, London.) Seals of different forms have been used for many centuries and carried the portraits, crests or some other form of identification of their owners. It was normal for the device to be engraved directly on to silver, but fashions changed in the late eighteenth century and many other surfaces were found suitable for the purpose, including jasper, agate and other semi-precious stones. Desk seals had handles, usually of wood or ivory, which fitted into a socket at the back of the engraved surface.

67 *Two seals*, English. (Victoria and Albert Museum, London.) The seal on the left dates from the late seventeenth century. The lid is set with an onyx intaglio. That on the right has a crystal set into the lid, and was made in about 1720. The handles of these seals form boxes in which sealing-wax could be kept.

68

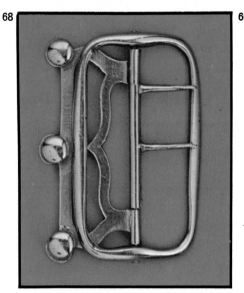

69

70

68 *Buckle* by Joseph Richardson Sr. (1711–85), Philadelphia. 1750–70. (Yale University Art Gallery, New Haven, Connecticut. Gift of W. M. Jefford) This small buckle, which is one and three-quarter inches long, is meant to be worn on a stock. Buckles were a necessity for use with the fashionable dress of the late seventeenth and early eighteenth centuries.

69 *Snuff-box* by Joseph Richardson Sr., Philadelphia. 1750–70. (Yale University Art Gallery, New Haven. M. B. Garvan Collection.) Whereas in former years the emphasis in American silver had been on form and line, in the middle years of the eighteenth century attention became fixed on detail and surface ornament. The old basic forms were lightened by flowers, foliage and rococo motifs. Joseph Richardson Sr. was a member of a Quaker family who produced a number of goldsmiths.

70 *Candle-snuffers and stand* by Myer Myers (1723–95), New York. 1755–6. (Yale University Art Gallery. M. B. Garvan Collection.) Myer Myers was one of the most prolific of American silversmiths, and this elegant pair of snuffers, with its stand, is a good example of his workmanship and fine understanding of the rococo.

71 *Two goblets from a set of six* by Paul Revere II (1734–1818), Boston. 1782. (Boston Museum of Fine Arts. P. Revere Thayer Collection.) One of the most popular figures from the American Revolution, Paul Revere was a competent engraver and prolific goldsmith. The interiors of these goblets are gilt. They were made for Nathaniel and Mary Tracy, whose initials they bear.

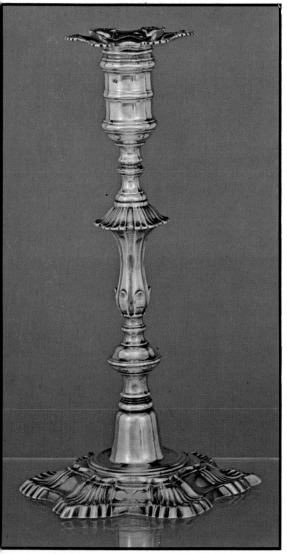

72 *Candlestick*, one of a pair by Myer Myers, New York, 1760–75. (Yale University Art Gallery, New Haven. M. B. Garvan Collection.) These candlesticks are executed in a well-defined, clear-cut style. The top of the stem is reminiscent of bamboo, a much-used feature of *chinoiserie*. The candlesticks are engraved: 'The Gift of Peter & Sarah Vn. Brugh to Cathae: Livingston'.

73 *Three panelled bowls*, the top bowl by Jacob Ten Eyck, of New York. *c.*1730. Left and right bear the maker's mark H.B., possibly for Henricus Bolen, New York. *c.*1690. (Henry Francis du Pont Winterthur Museum, Winterthur, Delaware.) The original purpose of the bowl is difficult to define although it is obvious that unlike the basket, it could hold both liquids and solids. Most of those surviving from the second half of the seventeenth century, such as the two examples illustrated here, derive either from the cup form or the basin.

74 *Pair of Candlesticks*, Naples. 1764. (Messrs. J. Christie, London.) In the everyday domestic silver of Italy, tastes changed little during the eighteenth century. Plain outlines and delicately contrived curves were sought after and were given grace and movement as the light caught and reflected from them.

75 *Tea-caddy spoons*, English. (M. McAleer, Barrett Street Antique Market, London W.1.) Until at least the middle of the eighteenth century tea was measured with the cup-shaped lid of the caddy. Tea-caddy spoons were not known until towards the end of the century; tea-caddies were small and therefore only the smallest of spoons could fit inside them. From the 1770s onwards caddy-spoons were made in increasing numbers and in a variety of shapes.

76 *Tea-caddy spoon*, London. 1892. (M. McAleer, Barrett Street Antique Market, London W.1.) Sometimes spoons for tea-caddies had handles of semi-precious stones; this example is made with a cornelian. The shovel-shaped bowl was fairly common.

74

76

77 *Tea-caddy spoons*, English. Above: Birmingham, 1890. Below: by Hester Bateman, London, *c.*1774. (Private Collection.) The Birmingham spoon has a shovel-shaped bowl and a mother of pearl handle; the Hester Bateman example is in the form of a shell. This, too, was a popular shape for such spoons.

78 *Pair of blue glass tea-caddies,* English. *c.*1770. (Private Collection.) These fine caddies are mounted in unmarked silver and have a red tortoise-shell case, also with silver mounts. The lids incorporate a silver-gilt cover overlaid with an elaborately pierced silver sheath which allows the gilt to show through. It was usual to have a decorative case for tea-caddies, the case fitted with a lock so that tea – still an expensive item – could not be pilfered by the servants.

79 *Sauce-tureen,* one of a pair by John Carter, London. 1774. (Private Collection.) Neoclassicism – the interest in Greek styles stimulated by the discoveries at Palmyra, Baalbec and Athens – swept Europe during the second half of the eighteenth century. Robert Adam was the greatest exponent of the style in England and his designs were copied and adapted throughout the country. John Carter was working for Robert Adam at the time he made the pair of tureens of which one is illustrated here, and it reproduces in all but the smallest details a design made by Adam a year earlier for a magnificent soup-tureen.

80 *Sauce-tureen* by Matthew Boulton and John Fothergill, Birmingham. 1776. (Victoria and Albert Museum, London.) Matthew Boulton's firm at Soho, Birmingham, manufactured silverware and ormolu in the neoclassical style, often using Adam's designs. This sauce-tureen is a fine example of the individual style created by Boulton's firm. The shallow fluting seen on this piece became widely used during the 1780s.

81 *Tea-caddies*, English. Left: marked HN, London. 1769. Centre: by A. Lesturgeon, London. 1778. Right: by Pierre Gillois, London. 1765. (Private Collection.) The caddy on the left is a typical example of those produced in the middle years of the eighteenth century; the influence of neoclassicism has not yet touched it and it is in the full rococo style incorporating *chinoiserie* motifs. The finial is in the form of a tea-plant. The caddy in the centre of the picture is in the neoclassical style, with clear-cut, unfussy outlines and delicate engraved ornament; the finial is in a classical Greek urn shape. The caddy on the right is also in the Chinese taste; a characteristic *bombé* shape chased overall with oriental figures and scroll patterns and having a reclining figure as its finial.

82 *Tea-caddies*, English. Left: by Hester Bateman, London. 1783. Right: by John Robins, London. 1796. (Private Collection.) The caddy on the left is decorated with festoons of flowers in bright-cut engraving. This is done with a special tool which gives a bevelled cut and at the same time burnishes the surface. This technique gives a crisp brightness which enhances the appearance of the silver and is immediately attractive. The caddy on the right is also decorated with this type of engraving, and the fluted panels add even further to the light, delicate effect.

83 *Soy-frame*, English. 1800. (City Museum, Sheffield.) Seldom found earlier than the last quarter of the eighteenth century, the soy-frame became a useful piece of table equipment in about 1800. This example is in Sheffield plate – a process of fusing a thin sheet of silver over a copper base, which was developed in 1743 and became immediately successful.

84 *Soup-tureen in the form of a turtle*, English. 1790s. (City Museum, Sheffield.) Of Sheffield plate, this tureen has a capacity of ten pints. The shell hinges upwards from the neck.

85 *Cheese-toaster*, English. *c*.1805. (City Museum, Sheffield.) This Sheffield plate cheese-toaster has six individual dishes for cheese, which was usually put on pieces of toast soaked in wine, and then grilled. The open hinged lid protected the hand from the heat of the fire and at the same time reflected the heat on to the cheese. There is a compartment for hot water beneath the dishes.

86 *Coffee-pot*, English. *c*.1760. (City Museum, Sheffield.) Until the early 1770s copper plate could be silvered on one side only; the interiors of hollow ware were either tinned or gilt. This Sheffield coffee-pot is of single-sided plate; the lid and foot are worked from two pieces of fused plate placed copper to copper, the upper layer of silver turned over to hide the copper edges.

84

83

85

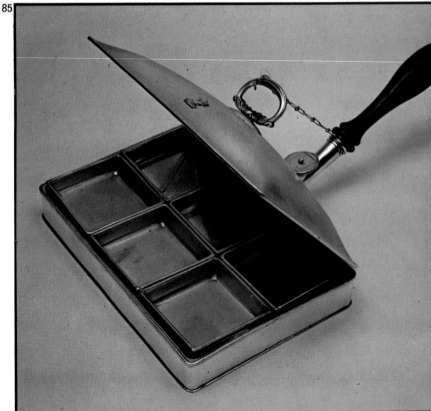

87

89

87 *Tea-urn* by Patrick Robertson, Edinburgh. 1770s. (Royal Scottish Museum, Edinburgh.) In the 1770s the New Town of Edinburgh was being built in the neoclassical style, and this style extended to all areas of the decorative arts. This urn was one of several magnificent pieces made in Edinburgh at this time.

88 *Three sugar-casters* by James Kerr, Edinburgh. 1730s. (Edinburgh Corporation Museum.) Scottish sugar-casters in general followed English patterns of style and decoration but were particularly notable for their simple, clean piercing and engraved ornament.

89 *Six silver brooches*, Scottish. Nineteenth century. (National Museum of Antiquities of Scotland.) Brooches were widely made in Scotland. There were two main groups: the plaid-brooch, which fastened the plaid over the shoulders, and the heart-shaped brooch which was used as a betrothal token. Many were set with precious or semi-precious stones or with coloured pebbles. The oval brooch set with an amethyst was given by Queen Victoria to her lady-in-waiting, Flora Macdonald.

88

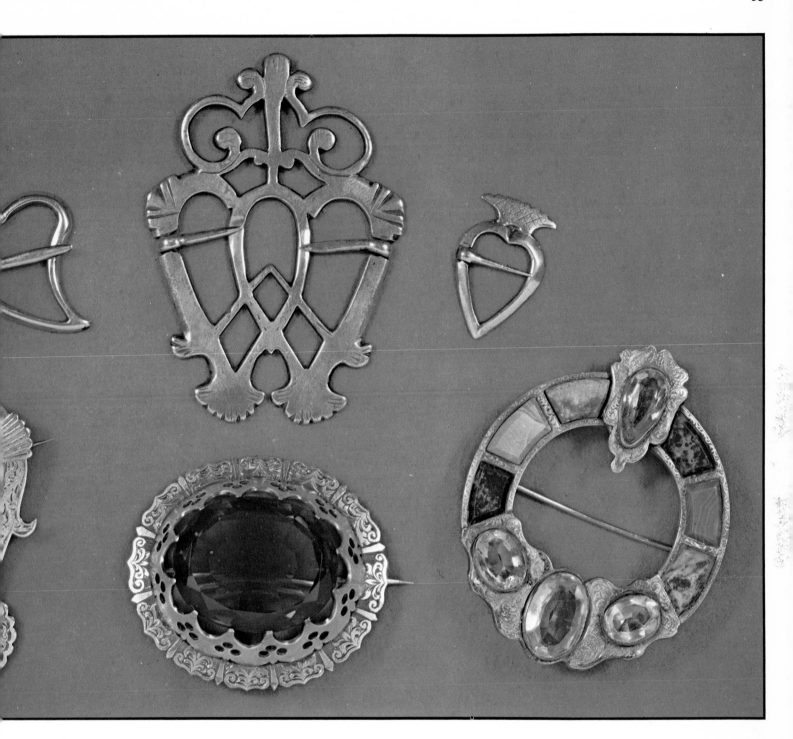

90 *Nef* by Henry Auguste (1759–1816), 1804. (Musée National, Malmaison.) Henry Auguste was the principal goldsmith of his day in Paris. He was goldsmith-in-ordinary to Louis XVI in the last four years of his reign and made some pieces subsequently for the Emperor Napoleon, among them this magnificent silver-gilt nef. It was made for the occasion of Napoleon's coronation, to the order of the City of Paris.

91 *Fruit-bowl and stand*, one of a pair by Paul Storr, London. 1810–11. (Wellington Museum, Apsley House, London.) This pair of silver-gilt fruit-bowls was part of the service of ambassadorial plate sent to Paris for the use of the Duke of Wellington. They are engraved with the Royal Crest and the crest of Wellesley.

92 *Tureen and cover* by Paul Storr (1771–1844), London. 1819–20. (Victoria and Albert Museum, London.) Paul Storr is considered to be the finest silversmith of the Regency period. The quality of his work is of the highest order and masterpieces of design and execution came out of his workshop by the score. This small tureen, only just over ten inches in length, has a massive effect which one would expect to find on a much larger piece. The fluted body is decorated with applied foliage and rests on scrolling feet.

93 *Tea-urn* by Paul Storr, London. 1809–10. (Victoria and Albert Museum, London.) Usually the tea-urn was used simply as a container for hot water, and the tea was made in a teapot or directly in the cup. It is supposed that such urns were also used for cold water in the dining-room. The spigot-handle was usually of wood or, as in this case, ivory. This urn carries a wealth of Greek and Egyptian detail in common with many other pieces of the Regency period.

94

94 *Basting-spoon* by William Fawdery, English. 1712. (Thomas Lumley, London.) Such spoons are thought to have been used in the kitchen for basting meat, but they could equally well have been used in the dining-room. From about 1690 basting-spoons normally took the form of the one in this illustration, with a large bowl and a long, tubular handle; in about 1715 this shape ceased to be made and thereafter such spoons were usually enlarged versions of the currently fashionable table-spoon.

95 *Caddy-spoon with cast bowl* by W. Pugh, Birmingham. 1807. *Caddy-spoon in the form of a hand,* maker's mark IS. c.1820. *Fish-slice with pierced and engraved blade* by John Younge and Company, Sheffield. 1783. The handle of the fish-slice by William Sutton. *Sifter spoon* by Joseph Taylor, Birmingham. 1802. (Private Collection.) The fish-slice was introduced in the eighteenth century, and was usually made in the form of a fish. By the end of the century it was common to find one in any set of silver tableware

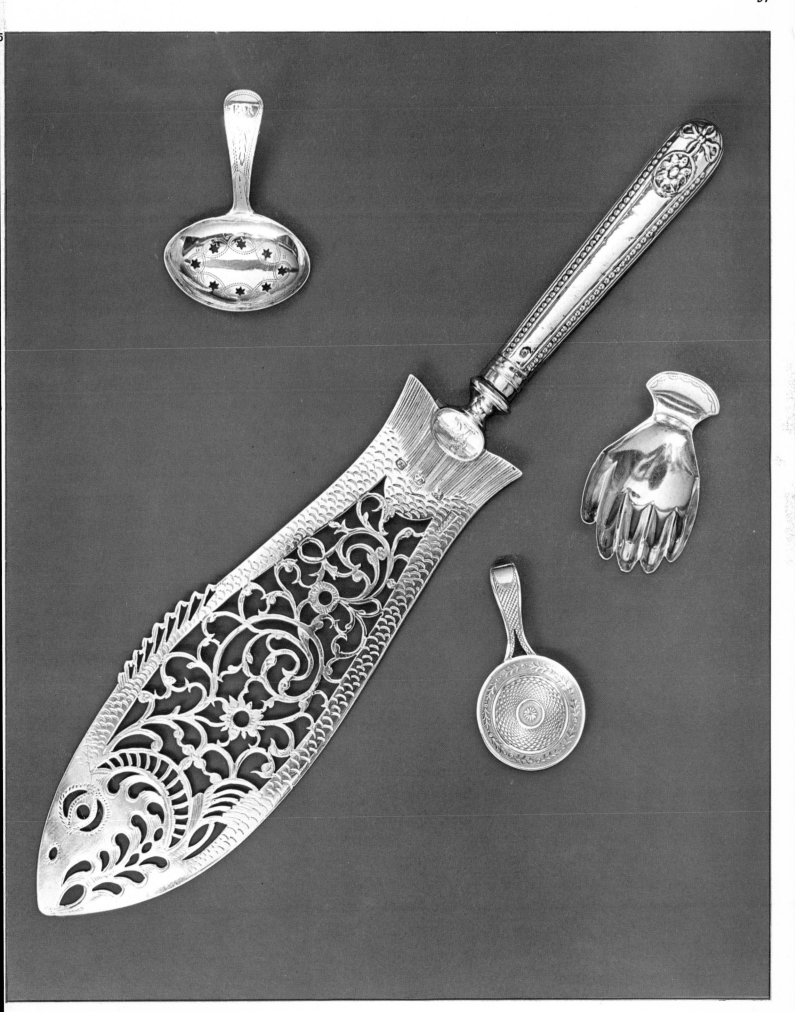

96

97

98

96 *Teapot*, Maker's mark SH, London. 1812–13. (Victoria and Albert Museum, London.) The general tendency in the field of domestic plate during the Regency period was towards lower, wider shapes. There was a widespread vogue for plate in these years and silver tea-services were a feature of every reasonably well-to-do household, also partly due to the reduction in the price of tea. This teapot is typical of those produced at this time; it has a wooden handle and an ivory and wood finial on the lid.

97 *Trafalgar Vase* designed by John Flaxman, made by Digby Scott and Benjamin Smith, London. 1805–6. (Victoria and Albert Museum, London.) Lloyds' Patriotic Fund commissioned Digby Scott and Benjamin Smith to make sixty-six such vases for presentation to those who had played an important part at Trafalgar. The vases were designed by John Flaxman, a distinguished painter and designer under whose direction many such monumental pieces of plate were made; he also worked for the firm of Josiah Wedgwood. The Trafalgar Vases bear the figures of Britannia Triumphant and a warrior slaying a serpent and the inscription 'Britons Strike Home'.

98 *Pair of sugar-vases* from a set of four by Benjamin and James Smith, London. 1810–11. (Wellington Museum, Apsley House, London.) Some sugar-vases were made in the second half of the eighteenth century; these are very late examples and formed part of the ambassadorial service used by the Duke of Wellington in Paris.

99 *Set of four coasters* by William Ealy and William Fearn, London. 1823. (N. Bloom, London.) Wine-coasters were made from the middle of the eighteenth century; they enabled unwieldy decanters and bottles to be passed from one diner to another with ease and without scratching the table. They were made with a variety of decorative detail but this set, left plain apart from the engraved crest, is typical of those made during the Regency. Most coasters have wooden bases.

100 *Teapot* by Edward Farrell, London. 1833–34. (Victoria and Albert Museum, London.) Edward Farrell is best remembered for the manufacture of this type of silverware; decorated with rustic scenes in an unsophisticated manner, his work was copied by many firms until the end of the nineteenth century.

101 *Butter-dish*, English. *c.*1845. (Sotheby's Belgravia, London.) The octagonal shape and elaborate decoration of scrolling leaves are characteristic of the pieces beloved by the early Victorians who, in their attempts to produce a rich effect, over-burdened their everyday domestic items with a profusion of ornament.

100

102

103

102 *Christening-mug* by Francis Higgins, London. 1865. (Sotheby's Belgravia, London.) Child-sized sets of a mug, knife, fork and spoon were fashionable christening presents from the early years of the nineteenth century. This is an ornate example in silver-gilt.

103 *Pair of double salt-cellars* by John Hunt and Robert Roskell, London. 1872. (Thomas Lumley, London.) The nineteenth century saw the revival of many earlier styles and designs. These silver-gilt double salts are interesting examples of neo-rococo work. The rococo was a style much favoured by the Victorians; it accorded well with their lavish tastes.

104 *Biscuit-box* by Elkington and Company, Birmingham. 1881. (Sotheby's Belgravia, London.) Made at the height of the vogue in England for things Japanese – prints in particular – this biscuit-box has areas of formal motifs framed by struts in imitation of bamboo. The hinged lid has a sunflower finial. It is thought to be an early design of Christopher Dresser.

105 *Tureen and stand* by Garrards, London. 1847. (Sotheby's Belgravia, London.) This melon-shaped soup tureen has a pomegranate finial. The gadrooned border is applied; the foliate handles and scroll feet are typical of the period. The engraved arms are those of Baroness Bray.

106 *Decanter* designed by William Burges (1827–81) and made by Richard A. Green for James Nicholson, London. 1865–66. (Victoria and Albert Museum, London.) The architect William Burges combined a talent for fantastic and wholly original design with a love of medieval metalwork. This decanter is a glass bottle mounted in chased and parcel-gilt silver, set with amethysts, opals, malachite and other semi-precious stones; it also incorporates ancient Greek and Roman coins.

107 *Christening mug* designed by Richard Redgrave R.A., made by S. H. and D. Glass. 1849. (Victoria and Albert Museum, London.) Designed for the Summerly's Art Manufactures in 1848, this fine cup was later shown at the Great Exhibition of 1851.

108 *Bowl* designed by C. R. Ashbee (1863–1942) and made by the Guild of Handicraft Ltd. 1895–96. (Victoria and Albert Museum, London.) C. R. Ashbee's Guild of Handicraft echoed the tradition of a small society dedicated to the non-capitalist principles propounded by William Morris. Ashbee's designs have a soft, discreet outline which speaks out against the mechanical harshness of earlier silverware.

106

107

108